PIANO ★ VOCAL ★ GUITAR

TOP COUNTRY
of 2016-2017

ISBN 978-1-4950-9093-6

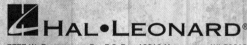

HAL•LEONARD®

7777 W. BLUEMOUND RD. P.O. BOX 13819 MILWAUKEE, WI 53213

For all works contained herein:
Unauthorized copying, arranging, adapting, recording, Internet posting, public performance,
or other distribution of the printed music in this publication is an infringement of copyright.
Infringers are liable under the law.

Visit Hal Leonard Online at
www.halleonard.com

BETTER MAN

Words and Music by
TAYLOR SWIFT

Moderately, in 2

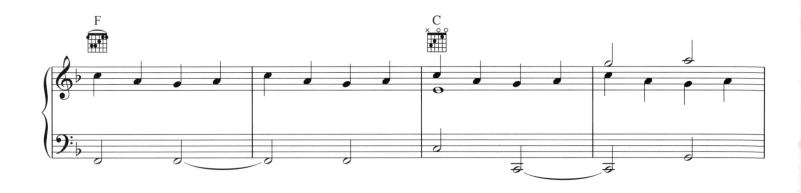

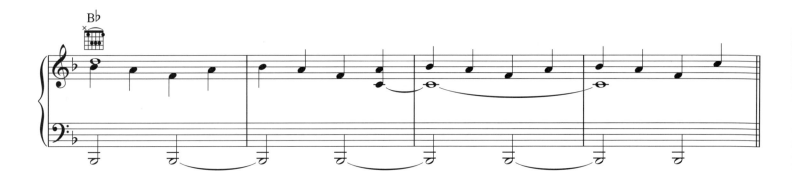

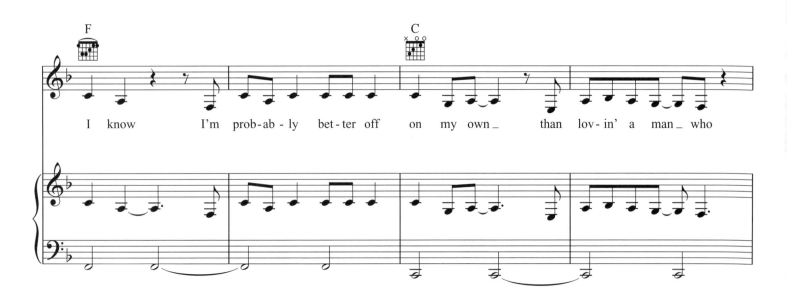

I know I'm prob-ab-ly bet-ter off on my own_ than lov-in' a man_ who

Copyright © 2016 Sony/ATV Music Publishing LLC and Taylor Swift Music
All Rights Administered by Sony/ATV Music Publishing LLC, 424 Church Street, Suite 1200, Nashville, TN 37219
International Copyright Secured   All Rights Reserved

BLUE AIN'T YOUR COLOR

Words and Music by HILLARY LINDSEY,
STEVEN LEE OLSEN and CLINT LAGERBERG

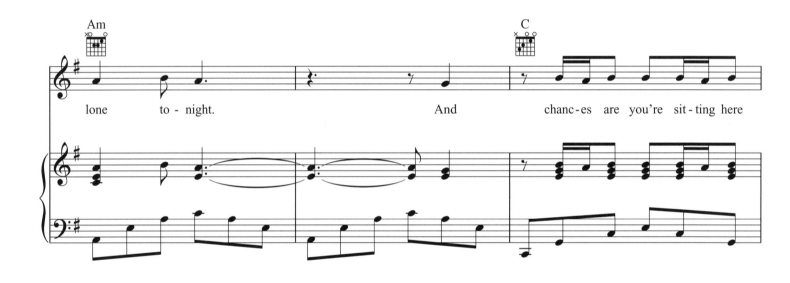

Copyright © 2015, 2016 HillarodyRathbone Music, We Jam Writers Group, Spirit Catalog Holdings, S.à.r.l., WB Music Corp., Music Of The Corn and House Of Sea Gayle Music
All Rights for HillarodyRathbone Music and We Jam Writers Group Administered by BMG Rights Management (US) LLC
All Rights for Spirit Catalog Holdings, S.à.r.l. Controlled and Administered by Spirit Two Nashville
All Rights for Music Of The Corn Administered by WB Music Corp.
All Rights for House Of Sea Gayle Music Administered by ClearBox Rights
All Rights Reserved   Used by Permission

FROM THE GROUND UP

Words and Music by DAN SMYERS,
SHAY MOONEY and CHRIS DESTEFANO

© 2016 WB MUSIC CORP., BEATS AND BANJOS, WARNER-TAMERLANE PUBLISHING CORP., SHAY MOONEY MUSIC, EMI APRIL MUSIC INC. and CDS WORDS AND MUSIC
All Rights for BEATS AND BANJOS Administered by WB MUSIC CORP.
All Rights for SHAY MOONEY MUSIC Administered by WARNER-TAMERLANE PUBLISHING CORP.
All Rights for EMI APRIL MUSIC INC. and CDS WORDS AND MUSIC Administered by SONY/ATV MUSIC PUBLISHING LLC, 424 Church Street, Suite 1200, Nashville, TN 37219
All Rights Reserved   Used by Permission

HEAD OVER BOOTS

Words and Music by LUKE LAIRD
and JON PARDI

I wan-na sweep you off your feet to-night. __ I wan-na love you and __ hold you tight, __ spin you a-round on some old __ dance floor, __ act __ like we nev-er met be-fore __ for fun. __ 'Cause

Copyright © 2015, 2016 CREATIVE NATION MUSIC, SONY/ATV MUSIC PUBLISHING LLC, RANCHO FIESTA PUBLISHING and SONGS OF SONG FACTORY
All Rights for CREATIVE NATION MUSIC Administered by SONGS OF UNIVERSAL, INC.
All Rights for SONY/ATV MUSIC PUBLISHING LLC, RANCHO FIESTA PUBLISHING and SONGS OF SONG FACTORY Administered by
SONY/ATV MUSIC PUBLISHING LLC, 424 Church Street, Suite 1200, Nashville, TN 37219
All Rights Reserved   Used by Permission

HUMBLE AND KIND

Words and Music by
LORI McKENNA

Recorded a half step higher.

Copyright © 2014 HOODIE SONGS
All Rights Administered by SONGS OF UNIVERSAL, INC.
All Rights Reserved   Used by Permission

MAY WE ALL

Words and Music by JAMIE MOORE
and RODNEY CLAWSON

May we all _____ get to grow up in a red, _____ white and blue _____ lit-tle town, _____ get a won't-

Copyright © 2016 BMG Gold Songs, Team Destiny, JMZL Music, Round Hill Works, Farm Town Songs and Big Loud Proud Crowd
All Rights for BMG Gold Songs, Team Destiny and JMZL Music Administered by BMG Rights Management (US) LLC
All Rights for Farm Town Songs and Big Loud Proud Crowd Administered by Round Hill Works
All Rights Reserved   Used by Permission

MY CHURCH

Words and Music by busbee
and MAREN MORRIS

Copyright © 2015, 2016 7189 Music Publishing and International Dog Music
All Rights for 7189 Music Publishing Administered by BMG Rights Management (US) LLC
All Rights for International Dog Music Administered by Downtown DMP Songs
All Rights Reserved   Used by Permission

SETTING THE WORLD ON FIRE

Words and Music by ROSS COPPERMAN,
JOSH OSBORNE and MATT JENKINS

Copyright © 2015, 2016 EMI Blackwood Music Inc., Songs By Red Room, Anderson Fork In The Road Music, Smackville Music, Smack Songs LLC,
WB Music Corp., Who Wants To Buy My Publishing, Jenkalenk Music and Atlas Music Publishing o/b/o Itself and Highly Combustible Music
All Rights on behalf of EMI Blackwood Music Inc. and Songs By Red Room Administered by Sony/ATV Music Publishing LLC, 424 Church Street, Suite 1200, Nashville, TN 37219
All Rights on behalf of Anderson Fork In The Road Music, Smackville Music and Smack Songs LLC Administered Worldwide by Kobalt Songs Music Publishing
All Rights on behalf of Who Wants To Buy My Publishing and Jenkalenk Music Administered by WB Music Corp.
International Copyright Secured   All Rights Reserved

SLEEP WITHOUT YOU

Words and Music by KELLY ARCHER,
JUSTIN EBACH and BRETT YOUNG

Copyright © 2016 by Downtown DMP Songs, Crack The Glass Songs, Wordspring Music, LLC, Super Big Music and Caliville Publishing
All Rights for Downtown DMP Songs and Crack The Glass Songs Administered Worldwide by Downtown Music Publishing
All Rights for Wordspring Music, LLC Administered by W.B.M. Music Corp.
All Rights Reserved   Used by Permission

SOMEWHERE ON A BEACH

Words and Music by ALEXANDER PALMER,
MICHAEL TYLER, JARON BOYER,
DAVE KUNCIO and JOSH MIRENDA

Lyrics: Bet you think I'm sit-tin' at home. Naw. Bet you think that I'm all a-lone. Naw. Bet you think I'm miss-in' you and wish-in' you would call my phone.

Copyright © 2015, 2016 BMG Silver Songs, Fuego Songs Publishing, Peertunes, Ltd., Jaron Boyer Music, David Ryan Music, The Brain LLC, WB Music Corp. and Music Of The Corn
All Rights for BMG Silver Songs and Fuego Songs Publishing Administered by BMG Rights Management (US) LLC
All Rights for Jaron Boyer Music Controlled and Administered by Peertunes, Ltd.
All Rights for David Ryan Music and The Brain LLC Administered Worldwide by Kobalt Songs Music Publishing
All Rights for Music Of The Corn Administered by WB Music Corp.
All Rights Reserved   Used by Permission

VICE

Words and Music by MIRANDA LAMBERT,
JOSH OSBORNE and SHANE McANALLY

Moderately slow groove

Sting of the nee-dle drop-ping on a vi-nyl. Ne-on sing-er with a juke-box ti-tle full of

heart-break. Thir-ty-three, for-ty-five, sev-en-ty-eight. When it hurts

this good, you've got-ta play it twice; an-oth-er vice.

All I'll

dressed up in a pret-ty black la-bel. Sweet sal-va-tion on a din-ing room ta-ble, wait-ing
wear a town like a leath-er jack-et. When the new wears off, I don't e-ven pack it. If you

Copyright © 2016 Sony/ATV Music Publishing LLC, Pink Dog Publishing, Anderson Fork In The Road Music, Smackville Music, Smack Songs LLC and Smack Hits
All Rights on behalf of Sony/ATV Music Publishing LLC and Pink Dog Publishing Administered by Sony/ATV Music Publishing LLC, 424 Church Street, Suite 1200, Nashville, TN 37219
All Rights on behalf of Anderson Fork In The Road Music, Smackville Music and Smack Songs LLC Administered Worldwide by Kobalt Songs Music Publishing
All Rights on behalf of Smack Songs LLC and Smack Hits Administered Worldwide by Kobalt Music Group Ltd.
International Copyright Secured   All Rights Reserved

WANNA BE THAT SONG

Words and Music by BRETT ELDREDGE,
ROSS COPPERMAN and SCOOTER CARUSOE

Moderate Country Ballad

Copyright © 2015, 2016 Sony/ATV Music Publishing LLC, Paris Not France Music, EMI Blackwood Music Inc., Rezolant Music,
Scrambler Music and Abbotts Creek Music Two - Divisions of Carnival Music Group
All Rights on behalf of Sony/ATV Music Publishing LLC, Paris Not France Music, EMI Blackwood Music Inc. and Rezolant Music Administered by
Sony/ATV Music Publishing LLC, 424 Church Street, Suite 1200, Nashville, TN 37219
All Rights on behalf of Scrambler Music and Abbotts Creek Music Two - Divisions of Carnival Music Group Administered by Bluewater Music Services Corp.
International Copyright Secured   All Rights Reserved

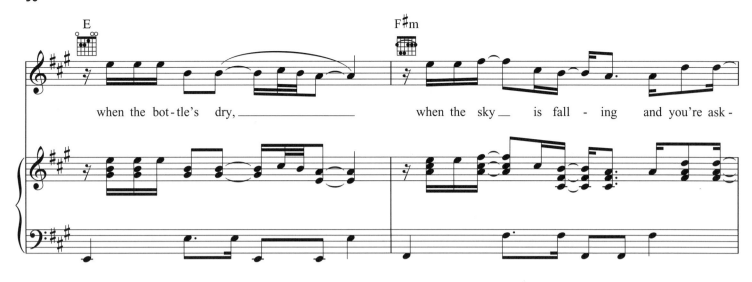

when the bot-tle's dry,_____ when the sky_ is fall - ing and you're ask-

- ing your-self___ why.___ Yeah.___ Oh,_ I wan-na be._____

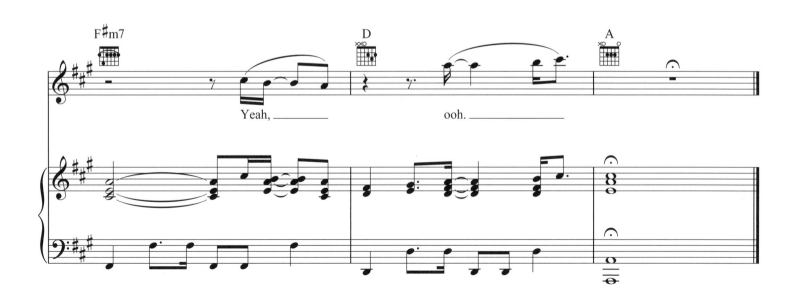

Yeah,_____ ooh._____

YOU SHOULD BE HERE

Words and Music by COLE SWINDELL
and ASHLEY GORLEY

Moderate Country Ballad

It's per-fect out-side,__ it's like God__ let me dial__ up the weath-er.

Got the whole__ crew here,__ I ain't seen__ some of them__ in for-ev-er.

It's one of those__ "nev-er for-get it, bet-ter stop and take it in"__ kind of scenes.__

Copyright © 2015 Sony/ATV Music Publishing LLC, WB Music Corp., Combustion Engine Music and Sadie's Favorite Songs
All Rights on behalf of Sony/ATV Music Publishing LLC Administered by Sony/ATV Music Publishing LLC, 424 Church Street, Suite 1200, Nashville, TN 37219
All Rights on behalf of Combustion Engine Music and Sadie's Favorite Songs Administered by WB Music Corp.
International Copyright Secured   All Rights Reserved

To Coda

ver it. And you know that if I just had one ___ wish, it'd be that you did-n't have ___

___ to miss this. You should be ___ here. You'd be tak-

- in' way too ___ man-y pic - tures on ___ your phone, ___ show- in' 'em

off to ev - 'ry-bod-y that you know ___ back ___ home, ___ and e-ven some you don't, ___ yeah. They ___

THE 1950s

50 country golden oldies, including: Ballad of a Teenage Queen • Cold, Cold Heart • El Paso • Heartaches by the Number • Heartbreak Hotel • Hey, Good Lookin' • I Walk the Line • In the Jailhouse Now • Jambalaya (On the Bayou) • Sixteen Tons • Tennessee Waltz • Walkin' After Midnight • Your Cheatin' Heart • and more.

00311283 Piano/Vocal/Guitar $15.99

THE 1970s

41 songs, including: All the Gold in California • Coal Miner's Daughter • Country Bumpkin • The Devil Went to Georgia • The Gambler • Another Somebody Done Somebody Wrong Song • If We Make It Through December • Lucille • Sleeping Single in a Double Bed • and more.

00311285 Piano/Vocal/Guitar $15.99

THE 1980s

40 country standards, including: All My Ex's Live in Texas • The Chair • Could I Have This Dance • Coward of the County • Drivin' My Life Away • Elvira • Forever and Ever, Amen • God Bless the U.S.A. • He Stopped Loving Her Today • I Was Country When Country Wasn't Cool • Islands in the Stream • On the Road Again • Tennessee Flat Top Box • To All the Girls I've Loved Before • and more.

00311282 Piano/Vocal/Guitar $15.99

THE 1990s

40 songs, including: Achy Breaky Heart (Don't Tell My Heart) • Amazed • Blue • Boot Scootin' Boogie • Down at the Twist and Shout • Friends in Low Places • Here's a Quarter (Call Someone Who Cares) • Man! I Feel like a Woman! • She Is His Only Need • Wide Open Spaces • You Had Me from Hello • You're Still the One • and more.

00311280 Piano/Vocal/Guitar $16.95

THE 2000s - 2nd Edition

35 contemporary country classics, including: Alcohol • American Soldier • Beer for My Horses • Blessed • Breathe • Have You Forgotten? • I Am a Man of Constant Sorrow • I Hope You Dance • I'm Gonna Miss Her (The Fishin' Song) • Long Black Train • No Shoes No Shirt (No Problems) • Redneck Woman • and more.

00311281 Piano/Vocal/Guitar $16.99

THE 2010S – 2ND EDITION

35 modern hits: All About Tonight • Better Dig Two • Cruise • Die a Happy Man • Girl Crush • The House That Built Me • Just a Kiss • Mean • Pontoon • Something in the Water • Stay • Take Your Time • Tennessee Whiskey • Wanted • You Should Be Here • and more.

00175237 Piano/Vocal/Guitar $17.99

Prices, contents and availability subject to change without notice.